LORD
OF THE SEASONS

Moving Forward through the Seasons of Life

CAROLYN VARGAS

WESTBOW
PRESS
A DIVISION OF THOMAS NELSON
& ZONDERVAN

Copyright © 2014 Carolyn Joan Vargas.

All rights reserved. No part of this book may be used or reproduced by any means, graphic, electronic, or mechanical, including photocopying, recording, taping or by any information storage retrieval system without the written permission of the publisher except in the case of brief quotations embodied in critical articles and reviews.

Edited by Pamela King

Front cover photo of Carolyn Vargas, taken by Ronnda Heinrich.
Author photo of Carolyn Vargas, taken by Asia Anderson.

Additional photos throughout book from THINKSTOCK.
Chapter 1, sundial, Jupiterimages/liquidlibrary/Thinkstock Chapter 2, cross, JanakaMaharageDharmasena/iStock/Thinkstock Chapter 3, eagle, Harry-Eggens/iStock/Thinkstock Chapter 4, rainbow, plusphoto/iStock/Thinkstock Chapter 5, tree, Ed Phillips/iStock/Thinkstock Chapter 6, clay pitcher, Sabine Schulte/iStock/Thinkstock Chapter 7, blossoms, Hirofumi Okubo/iStock/Thinkstock Chapter 8, baby shoes, aurorat/iStock/Thinkstock Chapter 9, gift, Natikka/iStock/Thinkstock Chapter 10, wheat, Jupiterimages/liquidlibrary/Thinkstock Chapter 11, walking into sunset, BERKO85/iStock/Thinkstock Chapter 12, sundial, Jupiterimages/liquidlibrary/Thinkstock Chapter 13, sunshine, Martin Lauricella/iStock/Thinkstock Last page of book, swan, Bas Meelker/iStock/Thinkstock

Scripture quotations marked *NKJV* are taken from the New King James Version of the Bible. Copyright © 1982 by Thomas Nelson, Inc.

Scripture quotations marked *NLT* are taken from the Holy Bible, New Living Translation. Copyright © 1996, 2004, 2007. Tyndale House Publishers, Inc., Wheaton, Illinois 60189.

Scripture quotations marked *NIV* are taken from the Holy Bible, New International Version. Copyright © 1973, 1978, 1984 by the International Bible Society

WestBow Press books may be ordered through booksellers or by contacting:

WestBow Press
A Division of Thomas Nelson & Zondervan
1663 Liberty Drive
Bloomington, IN 47403
www.westbowpress.com
1 (866) 928-1240

Because of the dynamic nature of the Internet, any web addresses or links contained in this book may have changed since publication and may no longer be valid. The views expressed in this work are solely those of the author and do not necessarily reflect the views of the publisher, and the publisher hereby disclaims any responsibility for them.

Any people depicted in stock imagery provided by Thinkstock are models, and such images are being used for illustrative purposes only. Certain stock imagery © Thinkstock.

ISBN: 978-1-4908-2993-7 (sc)
ISBN: 978-1-4908-2992-0 (hc)
ISBN: 978-1-4908-2994-4 (e)

Library of Congress Control Number: 2014904851

Printed in the United States of America.

WestBow Press rev. date: 4/10/2014

Contents

Introduction xi
Chapter 1   Lord of the Seasons 1
Chapter 2   Wondrous Gift 11
Chapter 3   Blessed Is the Man 19
Chapter 4   Rainbow's End 29
Chapter 5   Winter Winds 35
Chapter 6   Willing Vessel 57
Chapter 7   Spring 67
Chapter 8   It Wasn't Very Long Ago 75
Chapter 9   Blessings 81
Chapter 10   Seasons of Life 89
Chapter 11   I Will Say Farewell 97
Chapter 12   For a Brief Moment 103
Chapter 13   Glory 109
Final Thoughts 113

Dedication

This book is dedicated to a special circle of friends, loved ones, and prayer warriors who have stood with me and prayed faithfully for me during the most difficult season I have walked through. Thank you with all my heart. You mean so much to me.

Special Thanks

I would like to give special thanks to my longtime friend Pam King, who was willing to use her great talent to edit this manuscript. Words can't express my appreciation for your help. Thank you so much for all the many hours spent. What a blessing your friendship is to my life.

To everything there is a season,
a time for every purpose under heaven.
—Ecclesiastes 3:1 (NKJV)

Introduction

My beloved grandfather was a newspaperman. He owned his own newspaper and wrote a book, so the gift of writing is a part of my family heritage. Personally, I have never felt that I had such a talent. In reality, during high school and college, writing was a real effort for me, and I struggled. When I had something to say, I always felt more comfortable scribbling out my thoughts in verse and putting music to it, saying what needed to be said in song. How I didn't see that as writing all these years is humorous to me (and, I think, humorous to the Lord). As much as I don't see myself as a writer, I have been writing for years. Certainly, crafting a song is very different from writing a book, but they both have key similarities—they both convey what is in the heart to others.

One day in England, while working on my new album *Lord of the Seasons*, my producer and brother in the Lord, Mark Edwards, spoke up and said I should write some of the various stories that I had shared with him about my journey in life, my faith in Christ, and what had been my inspiration for the songs I wrote for the album. It really took me by surprise to hear him say something about writing. There were times when the thought of writing a book had crossed my mind. I even tried to get started a few times, but my efforts never got very far. Who knows what happened to those first efforts? No doubt, they were tossed out somewhere along the way.

I responded to Mark's suggestion by telling him I was no writer, and I proceeded to give him a list of all that I felt disqualified me. He appeared amused by my comments, and the twinkle in his eyes seemed to say,

"Yeah, right! Well, that is no real excuse!" He was not going to buy anything I said for an answer. I had seen that look before when working on some difficult vocals in the studio. It was a look that just spoke, saying, "I know you can do this." I laugh when I think of that moment now. Since that time, others have spoken nearly the same thing. And now, here I go, doing what I thought surely was not possible. Mark, you didn't know how prophetic you were! Thank you for that strong, substantial nudge in the Lord that finally got me started.

Today, I pick up that baton—that godly inheritance—and I will write what is in my heart. I am not an intellectual scholar or biblical theologian. I am a simple girl with a simple faith in God, having walked with Him since my childhood. I will write simply from the heart, and I pray that there will be wisdom, insight, and blessing for all those who read this book. I pray that something of what is written here will help unlock mysteries in the Lord, bring refreshment from the throne of God, and encourage you along life's journey.

CHAPTER 1

Lord of the Seasons

To everything there is a season, a time for every purpose under the heaven: a time to be born, and a time to die; a time to plant, and a time to pluck what is planted; a time to kill, and a time to heal; a time to break down, and a time to build up; a time to weep, and a time to laugh; a time to mourn, and a time to dance; a time to cast away stones, and a time to gather stones; a time to embrace, and a time to refrain from embracing; a time to gain, and a time to lose; a time to keep and a time to throw away; a time to tear, and a time to sew; a time to keep silence, and a time to speak; a time to love, and a time to hate; a time of war and a time of peace.
—Ecclesiastes 3:1–8 (NKJV)

Chapter 1

Lord of the Seasons

As the years grow in number, I find myself spending more time reflecting on life and the many passing seasons. I have seen changes in the world, changes in my life, and changes in the lives of many dear ones close to me. There have been so many experiences, stories to tell, great joys, and deep sorrows. Where have all the years gone? How could life be filled with such a rich variety of experience? I believe the writer of Ecclesiastes must have been pondering some similar thoughts as the words for chapter 3 were penned.

So much happens in the span of a person's years, from birth to the grave, this beautiful spectrum of life. These seasons of life are an interesting flow of the cycles of time. The understanding of time, like the Creator of time, the Lord Himself, is vast and has much more meaning than we can easily comprehend or explain. I will say this much though—God is eternal, and within eternity, He has created time for His divine purpose. How it all works together is part of the beautiful mystery of our God.

When we look at the surface of a person's life and reflect on times and seasons, we typically think in terms of years and what the cycle of those years represents from birth, childhood, and youth through to adulthood, followed finally in the completion of one's years, the end of a person's life on earth.

Even within the years, there are cycles—weeks, months, and yes, seasons. The easiest and most obvious way to think about time, and the seasons of life, is in the natural way. However, there is always so much more to a person's life than just what we see on the surface. We, as God's creation, are complex in design, and beyond the surface of natural chronological age are spiritual cycles and seasons.

Becoming more sensitive to what others and we walk through in life aids to bringing an understanding of the seasons and how these seasons of life build into the character of who and what a person is.

We often liken life and the seasons we walk through to a tapestry or mosaic—something beautiful that many seasons of life's experiences creates. Yes, these seasons will always bring change to our lives. There will be ups and downs, twists and turns, highs and lows. Some seasonal changes are neither good nor bad; they are just different and unexpected, and we are creatures of habit. We love our routines! We get used to things a certain way and find ourselves very uncomfortable and often disoriented with change. There will be change though, and if we want the new, fresh things the Lord has for us, we need to embrace the seasons and learn how to flow with these changes.

How we learn and grow through change will either enlarge us, deepen our character and faith, and mature us, making the tapestry of our lives even more beautiful and rich with color and hue. Or these very same changes can cause us to be broken, hard, and bitter. In that condition, life becomes nothing more than a dull existence, empty, and without purpose. That person's tapestry becomes dark and twisted, not something lovely and joyous to look upon and be blessed by.

If Christ is the Lord of our lives, He is indeed the Lord of the seasons as well. The Bible refers to the sons of Issachar, who had an understanding of the times (1 Chronicles 12:32). This wisdom, through understanding the times and seasons, aided them in knowing the best way forward for Israel. There may always be things in our lives that are a mystery and hidden from us—things that only the Lord knows and understands about the time and season we are in. But just as the sons of Issachar sought the Lord for an understanding of the times, this encourages us to seek understanding also, so that we too can walk in wisdom as we move forward through the seasons of life.

How do seasons come? Some come in the natural process of life—years come and go, and changes come and go. Some seasons slowly creep up on us, and gradually, the seasons change. Still other seasons come quickly and are completely unexpected. Suddenly, we realize that everything has changed seemingly overnight.

Some seasonal changes come due to life choices we make. Still other shifts and changes are thrust upon us due to the choices made by others. Sometimes, these shifts and changes are good. At other times, these changes are devastating, bringing disorder and great turbulence into the flow of life. We live in a fallen world; thus, not all of the choices made by others are as they should be. Whether good or bad, we will find ourselves impacted by the choices of others, and in the same way, our own choices will also impact the lives of those around us.

When we think about the shifts and changes of seasons, we must not forget that more is going on around us than we see with our natural eyes. Some seasons come by a divine shift of God in the supernatural realm. These types of seasonal changes affect our personal lives, but a greater plan is at work that impacts our world.

We understand that there is a real God, and there is also a real Devil. There is a real heaven and a real hell. There are real angels and real demons. The Lord is moving and working in our lives to bring about His will and purpose. All the while, our Enemy, the Devil, is relentlessly trying to disturb the flow of God's plan, striving to keep us distracted, get us off track, and keep us out of God's divine order, and out of season. The supernatural, unseen, spiritual realm is not make-believe or imaginary, like something from a fantasy movie. We must remain alert to the impact of the spiritual realm on this earthly, natural realm.

In talking about seasons, the most obvious way to relate this understanding is by the four seasons of the year: spring, summer, fall, and winter. We are used to understanding the natural seasons as being connected to specific conditions in the atmosphere that are either favorable or unfavorable for certain purposes. Farmers know when to plant seed, and it is not in the winter. We all know that we would not have the fireplace blazing in the middle of a hot 100-degree summer day. Learning to be more discerning of the season in which we live—not only physically, but also spiritually—can greatly increase the value of that season in our lives.

I live in Hawaii, and although our climate doesn't have extreme changes, we do have seasonal contrasts. The summers are hotter, and the winters are cooler and usually marked with more rainfall. Hawaii's climate changes are not as easily discernible for those who only visit the Islands, but those of us who live here are familiar with the subtle seasonal differences that occur throughout the year. What is interesting about the more subtle changes we experience is that time seems to coast along through the hot summer months; fans are set on high, and air conditioners go full-blast. Then one night you realize you need a blanket or two. It really didn't happen overnight, but it seems that way. The changes, while barely noticeable, had been occurring all around you.

Some of life's seasons come this way, in such a subtle manner that you never quite understand how you got there. At other times, these changes are more noticeable. However the seasons come, how we walk through them with the Lord will make the difference in the outcome of our own lives and the impact our lives will have on others.

With the fullness of Christ living in us and through us, there is joy and fulfillment in living. We have stability through all the seasons of life and a peace that goes beyond understanding. Our lives become something truly lovely, and we are able to bring these beautiful lives before a world that desperately needs His wonderful saving grace.

The God of heaven, the Creator of the universe, loves us with an everlasting love, and has promised that He will never leave us or forsake us. As we put our trust in Him, He will lead us and guide us through every season until we come to the end of our course on earth and transition from this natural realm into His glorious heaven.

The longer I live, the more I realize that life is good, as God is so good, and life is a precious gift and privilege to be lived for His purpose and glory. Every day is a special blessing, unique and irreplaceable. What we make out of each day has eternal value; we can be sure of this. We are writing history every day we live and during each season through which we pass. What will your story be? What will your tapestry look like?

Lord of the Seasons

Words and Music
By Carolyn J. Vargas © 2013/ASCAP

Lord of the heavens
Lord of the earth
You alone know the seasons of life
Lord of the heavens
Lord of the earth
You make everything
Beautiful in time

Lord of the heavens
Lord of the earth
You are the Lord of the seasons
You alone know the secrets of time
You are the Lord of the seasons

To everything, there is a season
To everything, there is a time
And a purpose under heaven
To fulfill the Lord's design

A time of birth
A time of dying
A time to plant
A time to reap

A time to tear
A time of healing
A time to laugh
A time to weep

To everything, there is a season
To everything, there is a time
And a purpose under heaven
To fulfill the Lord's design

A time to love
A time for hating
A time of silence
A time to speak

A time of joy
A time of sorrow
A time of war
A time of peace

Lord of the heavens
Lord of the earth
You are the Lord of the seasons
All creation gives glory to you
You are the Lord of the seasons

Lord of the heavens
Lord of the earth
You alone know the seasons of life
Lord of the heavens
Lord of the earth
You make everything
Beautiful in time

CHAPTER 2

Wondrous Gift

For God so loved the world that He gave His only
begotten Son, that whoever believes in Him
should not perish but have everlasting life.
—John 3:16 (NKJV)

For all have sinned and
fall short of the glory of God.
—Romans 3:23 (NKJV)

For the wages of sin is death,
but the free gift of God is eternal life
through Christ Jesus our Lord.
—Romans 6:23 (NLT)

If you confess with your mouth that Jesus is Lord and believe in
your heart that God raised him from the dead, you will be saved.
—Romans 10:9 (NLT)

Chapter 2

Wondrous Gift

I was about nine years old when I walked the aisle for Jesus. I would love to remember what song was sung as I walked forward, but sadly, I don't. It might have been "Just as I Am," as this song was often sung in those days at the close of the church service. What I do remember is that I wanted to give my heart to the Lord Jesus, and in my child's understanding, that is what I did that day.

My father was a minister and pastor of a small country church about an hour outside of Louisville, Kentucky. The church didn't pay enough salary for a living wage, so Dad taught school through the week. Every weekend, the family hopped in the car and drove down to the little country church, staying in the church annex. It was not an easy routine to keep up with, and I remember my grade school teacher being concerned about how often I would fall asleep at my desk on Mondays. Yet somehow, we got used to it and survived.

During those years, I heard stories of Jesus and the price He paid by sacrificing His own life on the cross for me so that I could be free of the burden of sin by receiving Him as my Savior. Many might believe that children are too young to make such a serious choice for their lives. But somehow, by hearing the stories of Jesus, in my child's mind and heart, I understood that I had sinned and that if I asked the Lord to forgive me, I would be cleansed, washed white as snow. I literally saw myself as a lamb that would be white, pure, and clean when I asked Jesus to forgive me of my sins and to come into my heart.

Saying a nine-year-old was a sinner brings up many questions, like how in the world could a nine-year-old be a sinner? I can assure you, I was a sinner, and I knew that I was, and I felt the heavy load of sin in my heart. I remember the weight of what I carried. I stole things out of the desks of my classmates at school. I cheated on a spelling test and felt no joy from the high mark I got on the test, so great was my burden. I stole a piece of bubble gum (priced at one cent) from Hudson's Market. As an adult, years later, I passed the place where Hudson's Market once was; it was all boarded up. Today, one cent is so insignificant that I could drop a penny on the sidewalk in front of what once was that store, and no one passing by would even bother to pick it up. But even as a child, I knew those actions were wrong and that penny bubble gum might just as well have been priced at five dollars, so heavy was my guilt and burden for having stolen it.

Oh, that wonderful day I gave my life to the Lord! My father baptized me. I felt so clean inside, as if a lamb of the purest white. The heavy load was lifted off of me. I had great peace. My heart was free. This lovely new life was the beginning of my personal relationship and friendship with Jesus Christ.

I was given a brand-new Bible that day, and while I was not a very good reader, I still made the effort to read. My new Bible was a symbol of the new life I had received, and I cherished it. I loved those thin tissue pages. I loved the smell of the leather as I held my Bible close to my face. All these many years later, I still love holding my Bible close to my face and heart, closing my eyes, and thanking the Lord for His precious Word and promises of hope on every page.

The years passed, and growing up in a preacher's family provided an interesting training ground for ministry. As soon as I was old enough to help out with something, I did it! From teaching Sunday school to singing special music, I was involved, and I did it with the passion of a young heart that loved Jesus.

Something happened in the process of those years that finally came to fullness in my late teens. I started to sense the plan of God for my life. One summer night, at church camp, I sat under a very large tree and looked up at the stars. Other campers were scattered around the campground, but I didn't pay any real attention to them. It was the end of the day, and soon we would hear the bell that meant all campers were to head back to the dorm for lights out. Until then, I had found a quiet, private place to meet with God, and I did!

I heard the Lord speak to me! You may ask, "How?" I don't really know what to tell you except that it was clear, although not audible. I had a quiet knowing that I heard the Lord call me to give my whole life to Him. I didn't quite know what that meant. What I did know was that I encountered God in a way that I never had before, and all that mattered was living my life for Him, wherever that might lead.

"Life recruit" was a term used that summer by camp leaders as they encouraged the young people to make a commitment of lifetime service to the Lord. This was especially aimed at those of us who sensed a calling on our lives for Christian ministry. Some young people felt they were to be pastors, while others leaned toward the mission field.

Carolyn Vargas

I was not aware that I had much of anything to offer God. I had no idea what He could possibly do with my life, but I knew I heard the Lord speak to me before the question was asked at the evening meetings. So when the minister asked the gathering of youth if there were any who felt the Lord was calling them to be life recruits, I knew I had to walk forward. I knew God called me to devote my whole life to Christian service, whatever that meant. That step launched me onto a road of great adventure.

Wondrous Gift

Words and Music
By Carolyn J. Vargas © 2013/ASCAP

Oh, what a wondrous gift
He gave on Calvary
All of His life for me
That I would be set free

No, it was not deserved
I should have died instead
His love/blood upon the cross
To pay my sinful debt

Broken in body
Bearing all my pain
That I would have healing
And peace that remains

Spilled out completely
His precious, holy blood
That I would live anew
In His redeeming love

What deep forgiveness
Poured out for you and me
Oh, what a wondrous gift
He gave on Calvary

CHAPTER 3

Blessed Is the Man

Blessed is the man who walks not in the counsel of the ungodly, nor stands in the path of sinners, nor sits in the seat of the scornful; but his delight is in the law of the Lord, and in his law he meditates day and night. And he shall be like a tree planted by the rivers of water, that brings forth its fruit in his season, whose leaf also shall not wither; and whatever he does shall prosper.
—Psalm 1:1–3 (NKJV)

The steps of a good man are ordered by the Lord, and he delights in his way.
—Psalm 37:23 (NKJV)

Blessed is the man who trusts in the Lord, and whose hope is in the Lord. For he shall be like a tree planted by the waters, which spreads out its roots by the river, and will not fear when heat comes; but its leaf will be green, and will not be anxious in the year of drought, nor will cease from yielding fruit.
—Jeremiah 17:7–8 (NKJV)

He gives power to the weak, And to those who have no might He increases strength. Even the youths shall faint and be weary, And the young men shall utterly fall, But those who wait on the Lord Shall renew their strength; They shall mount up with wings like eagles,
They shall run and not be weary,
They shall walk and not faint.
—Isaiah 40:29–31 (NKJV)

Chapter 3

Blessed Is the Man

Life is full of choices. Every day, we make so many that if we stopped for a moment to consider that, it would make our heads spin. What an overload of tiny decisions we make within the span of just a few hours. *What would I like for breakfast? What will I wear? Is it the white shirt or the green one?* You get the idea. More importantly, there are major life choices we make that will forever impact our lives and the lives of those around us. *Where will I go to school? What course of study will I pursue? With whom will I make friends? What job will I accept?* These are life-changing decisions, and each one needs to be made through sincere prayer.

As it is with most young people, when I was very young, I made most of my decisions based on what I felt was right. But I warn you, making decisions based on feelings can be very dangerous! Thankfully, and by the grace of God, since I became a Christian at a young age, I had a fairly strong moral compass, and that God-given moral compass helped to guide my decisions in a better direction. But as the years progressed, I grew to understand how important life decisions were, and I took these decisions much more seriously. I realized that if my life really belonged to Christ, then He had a wonderful plan. His plan included direction for my many life choices and ways to go forward even if I was boxed into a difficult corner.

Some of my learning came from just plain getting it wrong and seeing the disastrous results. At other times, thankfully, the opposite was the case. Whether from negative experiences or positive, lessons learned and applied can sure help to make the road much smoother and more easily navigated.

Scriptures like Proverbs 3:5–6 made much more sense as I grew in this understanding. I realized that God's Word, inspired by the Holy Spirit, was given to us as a reminder that life is to be navigated God's way, led by the Holy Spirit.

> *"Trust in the Lord with all your heart,*
> *and lean not on your own understanding;*
> *In all your ways acknowledge Him,*
> *and He shall direct your path"*
> *—Proverbs 3:5–6 (NKJV).*

Sadly, the world is full of people who elevate their own intelligence, reasoning, and human efforts above the knowledge of God and His Word. No, we don't check our God-given brain at the door. However, there are many situations in life when the answer to hard questions will not make sense to our reasoning or nicely fit into our logic. Making decisions from our best human thinking will fall short of leading us in the direction that is best for our lives and the impact our lives will then have on others. If we give the choice over to the Lord and ask Him to lead and direct us, even if the direction He provides seems completely opposed to our logic, then the right thing to do is to follow Him, trusting Him with the outcome.

Well, what if we get it wrong? We can sometimes think we were directed by the Lord, but we just miss it, and it wasn't the Lord's leading at all. Don't be discouraged!

God is just so faithful, and He loves us very much. He can help us make the best lemonade out of lemons! In fact, the Lord is so redeeming that He will give us beauty for ashes. To take that a little further, as one brother in Christ shared with me, the Lord is so redeeming that even when we encounter situations where things have gone very wrong, after the Lord works in the situation as only He can, it may seem as if the whole thing was always meant to be. But in reality, it is not so. I certainly agree! God is amazing! He will work all things together for our good. Those who put their hope and trust in the Lord will not be disappointed.

One of the most significant life choices I ever made was to move to Hawaii back in the 1970s. I was in my early twenties, had completed my degree, and was eager for what the Lord might have ahead of me. I really didn't have much of a clue as to what that might be, and then, through a series of circumstances, my path crossed with Bob Turnbull, founder and former President of the Waikiki Beach Chaplaincy. Bob asked me to prayerfully consider joining his staff and ministry team, and I agreed to seek the Lord for direction.

There was, however, a great deal more to becoming a part of the Waikiki Beach Chaplaincy staff than just moving to Hawaii. For one thing, I had to raise my own financial support. And just how was I going to do that? Oh, it is great to be young. Sometimes, these leaps of faith are much easier when we are young and childlike in our walk with the Lord. Not that I was completely blind to the significance of my decision, and not that it didn't take plenty of courage to make that huge step. I just had such childlike faith. I was completely convinced that my heavenly Father would take care of it all.

Carolyn Vargas

I earnestly prayed, and felt the Lord was directing me to make the move. However, there was a great variety of opinion when it came to the input that others freely gave about my decision, and what I should or shouldn't do. The conflicting advice actually was very confusing, and in many ways, rather upsetting for a young person trying to follow the Lord. Of course, there were some whose counsel I valued more than others, but in the end, it was a decision that I had to make on my own with the Lord. I sought the Lord the best I knew how. I pressed through it all with the strength the Lord gave me, and in the end, I felt strongly that the move to Hawaii to join the ministry of the Waikiki Beach Chaplaincy was indeed the plan of the Lord for my life.

This one life choice was so significant that I wouldn't know where to begin in sharing all that has come from it. For me, accepting Bob's invitation to join the Waikiki Beach Chaplaincy ministry team became a perfect example of just how important our life choices are. I will always be glad I made that decision, so firmly urged that it was the Lord directing me by the Holy Spirit.

I spent four amazing years in Hawaii, working with the Waikiki Beach Chaplaincy and growing in the Lord. In 1980, I married and left the islands to follow my husband in his career, but that is another story. Seventeen years after leaving, it became clear that my assignment in Hawaii was not finished, and in 1997, my husband and I made the choice to follow the Lord's direction and return to the islands.

I have written about the importance of the choices we make, but I would also like to chat about purpose. In order to better understand the seasons of our lives and make the right choices within each season, we need to be aware of our purpose in God.

I have found myself puzzled many times when I look at the lives of people who have so much potential and yet they seem to just drift along from one thing to another without any clear direction. Often, there can even be great worldly achievement. They live their lives; yet the lives they live are a rather shallow, empty hodgepodge of an existence, with no true value or meaning. They live focused on the natural realm, without any sense of eternity. They live according to what makes them feel good, what seems right to them at the moment, or what just sort of happens. Sadly, this drifting doesn't just occur among those who don't know God. For those who don't know the Lord, living in such a manner is not really surprising, but I have seen many Christians drift through life. They have never really discovered who they are, what the Lord has for them, or the significance of their contribution to God's eternal purpose. And so they drift.

Have you ever heard that old song, "Que Sera, Sera (Whatever Will Be, Will Be)," written by Jay Livingston and Ray Evans and recorded by Doris Day in the late 1950s? This drifting through life is a lot like that. Honestly though, there is nothing scripturally correct about "whatever will be, will be." Most of the things that "are" came about because of our choices. When we are able to recognize how valuable each day is and how short our lives really are, it will impact the significance and intentionality of how we live each day. This is not to confuse the issue of living a life of purpose with the idea that our lives are only some robotic, mechanical productivity for God. Rather, we are to understand

and embrace how valuable our lives are. Each day is a wonderful gift.

Clearly, our identity lies in simply being children of God, and that is enough—no strings attached. Our personal value is not in what we can do or accomplish for God, either. We are valuable to God just because He loves us. Still, having said all of that, our lives are full of amazing potential. If we never reach our potential, God will not love us less. However, awakening to what is possible with God living through us and directing our lives through the power of the Holy Spirit will stir up expectation. Our lives will then have a godly impact on the world around us. Blessing, favor, and fulfillment are all a byproduct of a life lived in God's purpose. The strength of our choices, made in light of the divine purpose of God, led by the Holy Spirit, will completely change the way in which we live.

Blessed Is the Man

Words and Music
By Carolyn J. Vargas © 2013/ASCAP

Blessed is the man
That walks with the Lord
That follows His command
That finds delight in Him

For he shall be like a tree
Planted by the waters
And in seasons of time
Shall bear fruit
He shall be like a leaf
That shall not wither
And all that he does
Shall be blessed

Blessed is the man
That trusts in the Lord
Whose hope is in the Lord
That waits on the Lord

For the Lord shall open
Up a path before him
For the Lord
Shall direct his steps
And he shall mount
With the wings of the eagle
And all that he does shall be blessed

CHAPTER 4

Rainbow's End

And God said: "This is the sign of the covenant which I make between Me and you, and every living creature that is with you, for perpetual generations: I set My rainbow in the cloud, and it shall be for a sign of the covenant between Me and the earth.
—Genesis 9:12-13 (NKJV)

So God has given his promise and his oath.
These two things are unchangeable because it is impossible for God to lie. Therefore, we who have fled to him for refuge can have great confidence as we hold to hope that lies before us. This hope is a strong worthy anchor for our souls.
—Hebrews 6:18-19 (NLT)

Let us hold tightly without wavering to the hope we affirm, for God can be trusted to keep his promise.
—Hebrews 10:23 (NLT)

Now faith is the substance of things hoped for, the evidence of things not seen.
—Hebrews 11:1 (NKJV)

Chapter 4

Rainbow's End

Disillusionment can come into a person's life for a number of reasons, but I have seen it manifest in the lives of many when they hit some very hard times. I have been there myself. The bottom falls out of life, and dreams are lost. Hope deferred makes the heart sick. The sea of hopelessness can cause a person to become so overwhelmed that they feel they are drowning. Life just didn't work out as expected, and suddenly, everything is questioned, even faith in God. The whirlwind and swirlings of the mind, will, and emotions are overpowering. The faith that once burned strong becomes a struggle, cold and empty. There may be an outward appearance that all is well, but inwardly, everything has shut down. The soul is in desperate need of an anchor. Fear not; there is hope!

Hope is a powerful anchor for the soul. It has held the *ship* of many lives through stormy waters. This anchor of hope is so strong that I have come to view it as the precursor of faith itself. Hope is not wishful thinking. It is a tangible, inner expectation—an unshakable anticipation that God is all that He says He is, and in Him, no matter the storm, His promises will prevail to bring you through.

Faith in God, I believe, goes beyond even the strength of the powerful anchor of hope. Where hope is the strength of tangible inner expectation, faith is the strength of tangible inner reality. Faith causes you to know, that you know, that you know without seeing with the natural eyes. You see with certainty with spiritual eyes that God is God, He is with you, and all is well. With that, you have an assurance of peace that passes all understanding, even through the darkest storm. It truly is a gift from God.

Storms can come in any season. Faith can be greatly tested through the difficult challenges of life that come suddenly and unexpectedly. No matter what we walk through, when we place our trust in the Lord, lean on Him for strength, and believe in the promises He has given, He will show Himself faithful.

The rainbow is a special reminder of God's faithfulness. It was a gift from the Lord after the great flood, and it is a symbol of covenant and promise. I love the beauty of rainbows, and in Hawaii, we see many. All the colors are lovely, and sometimes there are double rainbows. Those are very special!

While we know that the rainbow is a symbol of God's covenant promise, there are also many stories and fairy tales surrounding rainbows. We have all heard the old legend about the *pot of gold* at the end of the rainbow, and we know it is just a myth. But I think what people like about that story is that there is a place where dreams finally come true. While many people may think that a pot of gold is their dream come true, the truth is that there is much more to happiness than what can be found in financial gain or material possessions. Although there is no real pot of gold at the end of the rainbow, if we look closely, we will find treasure in the rainbow's significance and how it applies to our lives.

The rainbow often occurs after a storm. What have we learned through the storms of life? Have we learned to recognize what is really important? Do we value those things more than we did before? Have we changed for the better? Have we grown? Have we become more like Christ? Has our faith been stretched, our prayer life increased, and the fruitfulness of our lives multiplied? If we can answer yes to these questions, then we have obtained true, lasting treasure.

We have a covenant in Christ, with the God of all creation. As we allow hope to anchor us and faith to carry us, He will lead us through every storm. His promises are true. He is the Alpha and Omega, the beginning and the end.

Rainbow's End

Words and Music
By Carolyn J. Vargas © 2013/ASCAP

I'm searching for the rainbow's end
I'm reaching for a place
Where dreams come true
I'm searching for the rainbow's end
I'm waiting for the promise of my God

Shattered hopes and bitter tears
Disappointments through the years
What has happened to my heart
So deeply broken
So very hard

The journey goes on, day by day
I look into my heart and say
Do I still believe in you
And that your promises for me are true

I know that I will not let go
Although I struggle, there is hope
That your great hand
Will lead me through
Unto the place
Where dreams will then come true

All of His promises are true
All that He says, He'll surely do
I know that I can trust in Him
To lead me safely to the rainbow's end

CHAPTER 5

Winter Winds

Therefore whoever hears these sayings of mine, and does them I will liken him to a wise man who built his house on the rock: and the rains descended, the floods came, and the winds blew and beat on that house; and it did not fall, for it was founded on the rock. But everyone who hears these sayings of mine, and does not do them, will be like a foolish man who built his house on the sand: and the rain descended, the floods came, and the winds blew and beat on that house; and it fell. And great was its fall.
—Matthew 7:24-27 (NKJV)

Put on all of God's armor so that
you will be able to resist the enemy in the time of evil.
Then after the battle you will still be standing firm.
—Ephesians 6:11 (NLT)

Don't be afraid, for I am with you.
Don't be discouraged for I am your God.
I will strengthen you and help you.
I will hold you up with my victorious right hand.
—Isaiah 41:10 (NLT)

Chapter 5

Winter Winds

Looking back to the earliest of times, we see that winter was the most difficult season to live through. It required the most preparation to ensure survival. During other seasons of the year, people were focused on preparing for winter; seeds were sown, crops were grown and harvested, and supplies were stored. Thick, heavy garments were made to shield and protect the body through the long, cold winter days that were coming. Fuel was stockpiled to keep homes as cozy and comfortable as possible. Homes were checked and rechecked to make certain they could endure the harsh winter weather, and needed repairs were made with urgency. Preparations for winter were endless, for failure to prepare could well mean the loss of lives, and the clock was ticking. Winter was on the way.

Much has changed since the early days. We can now go to the grocery store year-round to buy our food. We go to shopping centers and purchase readymade clothing whenever we need it. As for our household fuel, there are very few people who still chop and use wood as the source for all their energy needs. Our fuel, whether electric, gas, or oil, is easily obtained.

Although we are grateful for the many modern conveniences of our times, little by little, we have become more detached from the overall importance of preparing for the winter season. Sure, we may run the car by the service station and have it winterized. We may even take a look over our homes to ensure that they are ready for the rough weather ahead. But for the most part, we continue living our busy lives, and whatever comes as winter arrives, we sort it out as we go along.

After all of that warm up I am sure you know where I am going with this. Yes, all that I have written about winter can apply to our personal lives, our relationship with the Lord, and the seasons of our lives.

I had lived through my own share of winters before—hard, bitter, cold seasons in which the struggles and trials were far more difficult than I ever thought possible. Those were dark, bleak seasons when God seemed far off; yet the need for connecting with Him was more important than ever. Winters can vary in degree and intensity. The harsh winters I had previously walked through seemed pretty intense at the time, but little did I know that I would come to consider them mild winter seasons in comparison to the one I had yet to face.

As most winters begin, the temperature starts to drop, and the wind chill increases. Then there are a few snowflakes that appear from heavy, dark skies. It is time to bundle up. Everything is about to change. And so it was in my life. It would be a blizzard such as I had never known before. Only by God's grace have I survived, and I am able to write about it now.

My marriage of thirty years was over! How was it possible? I don't know if I can find the words to fully express just how completely crushed I was. The heartbreak, deep wounds, and raw, piercing emotions left me at the bottom of an avalanche of overwhelming devastation. I was a completely broken woman. I had been dealing with some health issues, and although improving after surgery, I was not fully well when the avalanche hit. Already in a weakened physical condition, the emotional shock and trauma were severe blows to my health. I just could not seem to get stronger. It would be a slow and difficult journey to get through this long, dark winter.

Broken, oh, I was so broken. I cried constantly for days, weeks, and months. For the most part, sleep eluded me. If I happened to fall into a fitful sleep from sheer exhaustion, I would wake myself up crying; crying so hard that the sound of my own sobs awakened me. Then, as I realized I was alone, the pain seared into my heart in another jolting cascade, and I again sobbed uncontrollably. My stomach was a wreck. Anything I tried to eat made me ill. And my heart— I had never felt such heartache and sorrow. I thought my heart was going to burst open, the pain was so excruciating. I kept wondering how I could walk around and still function with all the emotional bleeding that was going on inside of me. The days became a blur of overwhelming anguish that continued for months and months.

Oh, how I loved my husband. I always thought we would grow old together and love each other into the sunset of our lives. I always thought that our love was special and the bond we had in Christ was unshakable. However, it had been shaken, and the bond was broken. We had been through hard times before. You can't be married for thirty years without going through a few things. I guess I thought, after all those years, that we had already gone through the roughest times. Now, in the second half of life, we were due to reap some wonderful, happy years together.

Sadly, things didn't go as I had always thought they would. In the end, I had to come to terms with the fact that I was not responsible for the choices that were made that broke our covenant, completely broke all trust, and broke my heart as well. If I were going to survive, I would have to press on alone and let go of the life we once had together, along with all the hopes and dreams we had shared.

How did it all get to this place? I can't even begin to tell you how my mind worked over the story again and again, trying to come to a different conclusion, but the ending was always the same. There was no way forward but through the long, dark tunnel. My prayers were reduced to desperate cries for help. I just didn't know how to pray. I felt such a need to connect with God on a deeper level; yet it seemed harder than ever to sense His presence, to feel His comfort, to gain His wisdom, to know He was with me, and even just to endure.

I had no strength left, in my weeping and despair, to do little more than utter, "Help, Lord, please help!" One day, as I cried and prayed in such a manner, face-down on the carpet, aware that I was even losing the will to live, I felt the Enemy laughing at me and mocking me, saying, "You won't get up this time. I have destroyed you."

With the little bit of strength I could muster, I said, "No, I will get up. My God will deliver me from all of this trouble." Inside, I felt no change or even any strength from the declaration I had made. I just tried to keep going, putting one foot in front of the other. Most of the time, it felt more like I was crawling, crawling through mud and slime. It was such a struggle. I was brought very low.

Long after the snow of winter stopped falling, the winter was still not over. There was the aftermath from the avalanche. I was pretty much snowed in, and it took a very long time for the snow to melt. I became much more isolated and withdrawn than was normal for the social

Lord of the Seasons

side of my personality. But it was needful as a time to draw close to the Lord and let Him tenderly minister to my broken heart and deep wounds.

I read every book I could find on how to heal a broken heart, applying what I could to my situation, and they helped a little. But my greatest comfort and healing came when I stood face-to-face with the Lord. As tears streamed down my face, He looked deep into my brokenness and ministered His healing balm to my bleeding wounds. I came to Him again and again. He *held* me and loved me, assuring me that He was with me, that He would never betray me, and that He would never leave or abandon me.

And then there were the *wolves* that I had to fight off. Sometimes, they came one by one, but most of the time, they came in packs. They always came in the same manner, during my most fragile and vulnerable moments. They launched their attacks during the lonely, dark nights—wolves of despair, depression, bitterness, fear, anger, self-pity, panic, and torment, just to name a few.

I thought it all had to be a bad dream and that one day, I would wake up, and the world would be right again, all back to normal. Unfortunately, nothing would ever be the same. I once had a little family—my husband, my dear daughter, and me. We were always the Three Musketeers—all for one, and one for all. Not having my little family as it once was has been a very great loss and sorrow to me, but it is the new reality that I must accept, and I daily trust God for the strength and grace to do so.

The day came when the final papers arrived. I looked down at the wedding ring I had continued to wear through it all, and I remembered our beautiful wedding day. I swallowed hard as I reached down and slipped the ring off my finger. It was finished. I was now a single woman. Tears filled my eyes as I asked the Lord to help me with this new life I was beginning, and I whispered, "More grace, Lord. I need more grace."

Winter comes, but thankfully, winter also goes. No season lasts forever. There is hope of the arrival of spring after the north winds cease to blow and the snow finally melts. The winter has been harsh, but through it, many lessons have been learned. Perseverance and endurance have been stretched through the trials and testing of adversity.

We all know someone who has gone through a dark winter season or perhaps is going through one now. I have several special people in my life who are fighting cancer even as I write. That is a horrific winter. Thankfully, I believe they are all going to make it. To God be the glory! Other dear friends recently lost their son. What heartbreak my precious friends have endured! Perhaps you are in a winter season yourself. Let me encourage you to keep going. You can make it! Don't give up! Find your refuge, strength, and comfort in the Lord, and He will bring you through the darkness.

I urge you to live a life that prepares you for all seasons, winter included. God is not a fair-weather friend. He will be there for you in the darkest of times.

We never know what is ahead on the road of life. As it is in the natural, so it is in the spiritual; we must be well prepared to survive winter. Let your roots go down deep in Christ. Develop a relationship of intimacy with the Lord. Build a sound and sturdy foundation on the Word of God. Abide in His love, remaining strong in the Lord and in the power of His might, and the Enemy will not be able to take you down in the winter season.

Surviving Winter

Encouragement for Those in a Winter Season

Fix Your Gaze on the Lord

> So we don't look at the troubles we can see now;
> rather, we fix our gaze on things that cannot be seen.
> For the things we see now will soon be gone,
> but the things we cannot see will last forever.
> —2 Corinthians 4:18 (NLT)

> Let us fix our eyes on Jesus, the author and
> perfecter of our faith, who for the joy set before
> him endured the cross, scorning its shame, and sat
> down at the right hand of the throne of God.
> —Hebrews 2:12 (NIV)

No matter what you may face in your winter season, if you are constantly focused on the difficult situation, it will swallow you up. Remind yourself to keep your eyes on the Lord. If you realize your gaze has shifted, get your eyes right back on Him.

Hold Your Savior's Hand

> I cling to you;
> your strong right hand
> holds me securely.
> —Psalm 63:8 (NLT)

> For I hold you by your right hand—I, the LORD
> your God. And I say to you, 'Don't be afraid.
> I am here to help you.
> —Isaiah 41:13 (NLT)

You may feel that you are closed in, with darkness all around, but remember that the hand of the Lord is there for you to hold. He will lead you through the darkness.

Rebuke Fear

> For God has not given us the spirit of fear;
> but of power, and of love, and of a sound mind.
> —2 Timothy 1:7 (NKJV)

Along with fear comes his brother, torment. The Enemy loves to use this pair to try to paralyze us. Don't let him!! God has not given you a spirit of fear!

Trust

> Trust in the LORD with all your heart; and
> lean not unto your own understanding.
> In all your ways acknowledge him, and
> he shall direct your paths.
> —Proverbs 3:5-6 (NKJV)

> Do not be anxious about anything, but
> in everything, by prayer and petition, with
> thanksgiving, present your requests to God.
> —Philippians 4:6 (NIV)

When you face a mountain of trouble, it seems harder than ever to let go and simply trust in the Lord. We seem driven to do things to solve our own problems. And there are certainly times when the Lord will direct us to do certain things as a part of His plan for our deliverance. But many times, we are to be still and at peace, letting God work out His plan for us in His way and in His timing. Letting go of control is not an easy thing, but remember, Father always knows best. Give it up, and trust the Lord!

Prayer

> Pray without ceasing.
> —1 Thessalonians 5:17 (NKJV)

We definitely want to raise the bar on our prayer life during winter seasons. This should go without saying, but sometimes we become so overwhelmed that we end up shutting down our prayer life, and this just won't bring the victory we need. It's important to persevere in prayer.

Those who usually have a morning prayer time might consider adding an evening prayer time as well. But don't limit the times and ways you can pray and meet with the Lord. It doesn't always have to be at your home, on your knees. Along with those special times you set aside, become more aware of opportunities throughout the day when you might commune with the Lord, even as you come and go. I love walking with the Lord in the cool of the day, just as the sun is setting. As we walk along, we talk and fellowship, just as friends would. So, if you catch yourself worrying, flip that around and pray!

Carolyn Vargas

The Word of God

> For the word of God is living, and powerful, and sharper than any two-edged sword, piercing even to the dividing asunder of soul and spirit, and of the joints and marrow, and is a discerner of the thoughts and intents of the heart.
> —Hebrews 4:12 (NKJV)

The Word of God is full of power! Search out those special Scriptures that encourage you to keep pressing on in spite of whatever you might be going through and that remind you that your hope is in the Lord.

Also, search the Bible for Scriptures that might not be as familiar to you but have to do with your need and situation—Scriptures that pertain to health, finances, or relationships. Write them down. Put them around the house or on a card in your pocket or purse. Read them. Speak them out loud. Meditate on them, and pray them. Let the Word of God minister to you.

Weed the Garden

> For verily I say unto you,
> That whosoever shall say unto this mountain,
> Be removed, and be cast into the sea;
> and shall not doubt in his heart,
> but shall believe that those things
> which he said shall come to pass;
> he shall have whatsoever he said.
> —Mark 11:23 (NKJV)

> If any of you lacks wisdom, he should ask God,
> who gives generously to all without finding fault,
> and it will be given to him. But when he asks,
> he must believe and not doubt,
> because he who doubts is like a wave of the
> sea, blown and tossed by the wind.
> That man should not think he will
> receive anything from the Lord;
> he is a double-minded man,
> unstable in all he does.
> —James 1:5–8 (NIV)

Get rid of the weeds of doubt and unbelief that may be intruding into your thoughts and heart. These are faith destroyers. Sometimes we become so used to the weeds of doubt and unbelief that we are not aware that they are working in our lives. They might be hard to recognize, but ask the Lord to help you identify them, and He will do it.

Forgiveness

> And when you stand praying, if you hold anything
> against anyone, forgive him, so that your Father
> in heaven may forgive you your sins.
> —Mark 11:25 (NIV)

> Be kind and compassionate to one another,
> forgiving each other, just as in Christ
> God forgave you.
> —Ephesians 4:32 (NIV)

As we press through a winter season, the Lord may reveal to us that there are people we need to forgive. Forgiveness doesn't mean excusing someone's ungodly behavior or subjecting yourself to abusive behavior. Forgiveness is unmerited grace, and just as the Lord forgave us with unmerited grace, we forgive others.

We may have already gone through the process of forgiving someone; yet a thought or the mention of that person's name stirs up strong emotions all over again. Don't be discouraged; some situations require us to continue forgiving, especially if there are ongoing situations we must deal with.

Also, there may be layers of forgiveness that we need to work through. That doesn't mean that we were not sincere in our earlier efforts to forgive. There may be deeper places in our hearts that the Lord wants to touch, calling upon us to forgive at a deeper level. Sometimes we are only able to see what our emotions are ready to handle, and as the Lord brings healing to our wounds, we can see more.

Lighten Up

> A merry heart does good like a medicine:
> but a broken spirit dries the bones.
> —Proverbs 17:22 (NKJV)

Winter seasons can be pretty intense times. Don't lose your sense of humor in the midst of what you are going through. The Scriptures tell us that a merry heart does us good like a medicine. Science is now confirming what was written in the Bible so many years ago. A good belly laugh releases beneficial chemicals into the body. I like to call them *feel-good* or *happy* hormones. Science calls them endorphins. So, laugh a little; in fact, laugh a lot! It's good for you.

Rest

> Then, because so many people were coming and going that they did not even have a chance to eat, he said to them, "Come with me by yourselves to a quiet place and get some rest."
> —Mark 6:31 (NIV)

When going through difficult trials, we need to recharge our batteries more than we would under normal circumstance. Remember good food and exercise. Also, give yourself permission to rest. Put your feet up! Watch an enjoyable, uplifting movie; read a book; or find your bed and give yourself permission to sleep. During great stress and crisis, our physical bodies need extra care.

Support

> There are "friends" who destroy each other,
> but a real friend sticks closer than a brother.
> —Proverbs 18:24 (NLT)
>
> A friend loves at all times,
> and a brother is born for adversity.
> —Proverbs 17:17 (NIV)

We were never created to live life alone. We need each other. Don't be afraid to reach out to others in your difficult seasons and ask for help and support. But be wise as to who you share your burdens with and who you allow to speak into the situations in your life. We all have acquaintances—people we know superficially—but then there are those we know on a deeper level. Those who have proven themselves to be loyal, trustworthy, full of faith, and full of the Word of the Lord are those who will have your best interest at heart.

Depending on your situation, you may find a support group to be of great help. Or you may need pastoral or professional counseling.

Whatever your need is, just know that there are people who can help. You are not alone. The Lord is with you, and He has many sons and daughters available to help you in your time of need.

One Day at a Time

> So don't worry about tomorrow,
> for tomorrow will bring its own worries.
> Today's trouble is enough for today.
> —Matthew 6:34 (NIV)

In the midst of the winter season, it is important to remember to take just one day at a time! It may seem like you aren't moving forward, but sometimes, simply getting through the day is a great victory.

Reach Out To Others

> In the same way, let your light shine before men,
> that they may see your good deeds and
> praise your Father in heaven.
> —Matthew 5:16 (NIV)

> Do to others as you would have them do to you.
> —Luke 6:31 (NIV)

> And if anyone gives even a cup of cold water to one of these little ones because he is my disciple, I tell you the truth, he will certainly not lose his reward.
> —Matthew 10:42 (NIV)

> Each of you should look not only to your own interests, but also to the interests of others.
> —Philippians 2:4 (NIV)

Make an effort to set aside your own personal struggle, and reach out to someone else. There are people in your life who are going through difficult times. As others have reached out to you, do likewise. Don't underestimate the value of even the smallest gesture. Send out a card, make a phone call, or offer a prayer. Bring encouragement to someone else. It will lift up your own heart as well.

Atmosphere

> For we wrestle not against flesh and blood,
> but against principalities, against powers,
> against the rulers of the darkness of this world,
> against spiritual wickedness in heavenly places.
> —Ephesians 6:12, (NKJV)

There is a lot going on in the unseen realm around us. Be aware of that, and make every effort to create an atmosphere of heaven in your home. Play worship music and recordings of the Bible. Pray in every room, and dedicate your home to the Lord. Your home is to be a haven of rest, a place of peace. Declare safe boundaries and the Lord's angelic protection over and around your property. Be careful what you allow to enter your home through media—television, computers, music, books, magazines, etc.—as well as through other avenues, such as drugs and abusive practices. The Enemy will take advantage of any open door. It is important that you give him *no access!*

Worship

> Ascribe to the LORD the glory due his name;
> worship the LORD in the splendor of his holiness.
> —Psalm 29:2 (NIV)

> O come, let us worship and bow down:
> let us kneel before the LORD our maker.
> —Psalm 95:6 (NKJV)

Lift up your hands, and give the Lord the worship that is due Him. Sing to Him a new song! Rejoice in the Lord your God! Our worship to the Lord is not conditional on our circumstances; we worship because He is worthy of all glory and worthy of all praise! In the midst of your worship, you will find yourself refreshed in His presence.

The Battle Is the Lord's

> He said: "Listen, King Jehoshaphat and
> all who live in Judah and Jerusalem!
> This is what the LORD says to you:

> 'Do not be afraid or discouraged because of this
> vast army. For the battle is not yours, but God's ...
> You will not have to fight this battle.
> Take up your positions; stand firm and see
> the deliverance the LORD will give you,
> O Judah and Jerusalem. Do not be afraid;
> do not be discouraged. Go out to face them
> tomorrow, and the LORD will be with you."
> —2 Chronicles 20:15, 17 (NIV)

> Therefore put on the full armor of God,
> so that when the day of evil comes,
> you may be able to stand your ground,
> and after you have done everything, to stand.
> —Ephesians 6:13 (NIV)

In the end, out of all that you do to gain victory and overcome in a very difficult winter season, one of the most important things to remember is that the battle belongs to the Lord. Do what the Lord shows you to do, and then stand firm. The Lord is with you!

Winter Winds

Words and Music
By Carolyn J. Vargas © 2013/ASCAP

The winter winds
Now blow again
It's time to light the fire
And stay inside

Dark, weary skies
Days slipping by
Such empty feelings
Whisper in my mind

Winter can test us
Like no other season
The long, dark night of the soul
Help me to trust
In your purpose and your reason
Deep hidden ways
As winter winds blow

The winter winds
Now blow again
It's time for resting
And for staying warm
Slow, easy days
To gather strength
Finding comfort wrapped
Within your arms

Help me to know
There is no wasted season
No matter what I see
As I trust in your purpose
And your reason
I am prepared
For what you have for me

The winter winds
Now blow again
Yet in your shelter
There is hope and ease
Days of love
Days of joy
As you flood me with your
Grace and peace

You remind me
No season lasts forever
As you work deep inside
Yielding to you
Determines all that matters
When you will change
The season of my life

Please hold me close
As winter winds blow

CHAPTER 6

Willing Vessel

Even in old age they will still produce fruit;
they will remain vital and green.
—Psalm 92:14 (NLT)

I will be your God throughout your lifetime—
until your hair is white with age.
I made you, and I will care for you.
—Isaiah 46:4 (NLT)

We will not hide these truths from our children;
we will tell the next generation
about the glorious deeds of the lord,
about his power and his mighty wonders.
—Psalm 78:4 (NLT)

Satisfy us in the morning with your unfailing love,
that we may sing for joy and be glad all our days.
—Psalm 90:14 (NIV)

Chapter 6

Willing Vessel

One of the great advantages of living through the many seasons of life is the perspective, insight, and wisdom we gain through the journey. From the youngest to the oldest, God has a wonderful plan for each one of us, and it is very important that we not lose sight of that in this changing world.

In our culture, properly seeing and celebrating the value and uniqueness of each person's life can sometimes get cloudy. Each person is valuable and precious to the Lord, but we are not always aware of how greatly we have been influenced by the thinking of the world as to how we determine value. We live in a world that focuses on the superficial, on the outward appearance, and especially youth and beauty—the Hollywood version of life. This trend has woven and embedded its way into our lives to the point where many of our dear young people now believe their own personal worth and value is measured by this standard.

Youth and beauty are so glamorized and glorified that, in many cases, a troubling disconnect between the generations and a devaluing of elders have emerged. Our young people have lost much of the respect and honor that was once given to the older generation. The respect and appreciation that was once shown to the elders that worked endlessly to give the younger generation a *leg up* in life has all but vanished! The sacrifices that have been made to clear obstacles from the paths of young people are often taken for granted. Rather than recognizing all that their elders have done to encourage and equip them to go further than their elders could have ever hoped to go themselves, many young people look at life as if everyone owes them something. This sense of entitlement is concerning.

Sadly, many of these same symptoms are cropping up in the church—the very place where what is in the heart, not the outward appearance, should be emphasized. In the very place where elders should be honored and valued, they are often set aside as old relics that don't get it and have outlived their usefulness for the Lord and the body of Christ.

It grieves me when I see preferences being made to maintain a certain *image* in the church. In order to attract a particular type of people, emphasis is placed on outward appearance and style, outweighing the value of character, inward beauty, and anointing.

There are too many sad stories about people who were happily serving in their church and then suddenly were told they were no longer needed. There was never a question of their moral character, steadfast devotion to God and ability to serve in the position. The changes were made because of a certain image the church wanted to portray.

The fruit of young leaders taking the reins of the church prematurely, when they have not yet had the depth of seasoning and experience to be able to handle the many challenges they will face, yields poor results in most cases. At best, premature leadership has contributed to producing a more carnal, superficial church. At worst, some of these dear young leaders, who in no way were prepared for the load they took on, have fallen from the faith completely and taken many down with them.

Lord of the Seasons

This trend of not valuing the older members of the body of Christ can also work in reverse, although I haven't seen it nearly as much. In such cases, there is no place made for the young people of the church to work alongside their elders, grow, and be raised up to the places the Lord has for them. Their contribution isn't valued. Thus, they never gain the experience they need and don't develop their gifts. They don't have the opportunity to be strengthened through the wisdom of working alongside mature Christians who can help them grow and navigate well through the many challenges they might face while maintaining steady growth and godly character.

No scenario is ever *one-size-fits-all*. Chronological age doesn't always equate with spiritual maturity, and even when patterns surface, there are always varying degrees. Thankfully, these stories of devaluing certain groups in the body of Christ don't apply everywhere. Still, as we go forward with the Lord, we need to remain alert to the schemes of the Enemy and seek the Lord for wisdom concerning these matters. We need one another in order to fulfill the plan of God.

I believe a healthy church is a multigenerational church. The zeal and passion of the young and the experience, maturity, and wisdom of the older ones are to link arms and work together. There is great value in what both have to give, and working together produces multiplied fruitfulness.

I love young people. I love talking with them, getting to know them, hearing the stories of how they came to know Christ, and being stirred by their contagious zeal for the things of God. I am eager to see younger generations rise up and take their place in the body of

Christ in devotion, passion, and dedication to seeing the gospel of Christ ministered around the world. I eagerly cheer them on. But just one segment of the body of Christ can't do it alone. We need the whole body of Christ working together—young, old, and everything in between, not one or the other.

Regardless of what age group we find ourselves in, our Enemy, the Devil, is always trying to convince us to drop out of the race. I have had my share of moments when I questioned whether or not my best years were behind me. I have the scars of many battles. I have fought my share of spiritual wars. In recent years, I have struggled with health issues and difficult vocal problems. Then when I went through menopause, a whole new group of challenges showed up that I had to trust God to help me overcome. One of which was that I found myself forgetting the words to songs as I was singing them. This is not a good thing, since one of the areas where the Lord has used me the most is in the area of music and worship. There were times when I thought it would be easier to just fade into the sunset and let the young ones carry the weight of things rather than continue to fight the battles. I thought, *Well, I did my bit; now it is their turn!* Funny, though—I never felt the Lord agreed with it. *Ha!*

Instead, the Lord made it clear to me that He wasn't discontinuing His plans for my life just because I was in the second half of it. I was reminded of the strong sense of *destiny in the Lord* that I had always walked in and of the things not yet fulfilled that the Lord had spoken to me about through the years. There were still songs to write and songs to sing. There were things that the Lord taught me along the journey that needed to be passed on to others. Most of all, I had not lost my *roar*. How

Lord of the Seasons

could I just fade into the sunset? I realized how much the Lord wanted to hear the young lions and old lions roar together, for His glory.

So I let go of all that silly thinking, that perhaps I too had outlived my usefulness for God. Instead, I renewed my dedication to the purpose of God for the second half of life, offering my willingness that He use my life. I asked Him to stir up the gifts within me and release upon my life fresh vision. I felt the Lord was pleased.

One Sunday morning, the Lord had a surprise for me. I was in a church service where the guest speaker was a lovely woman in her eighties. This woman is a missionary to India and travels the globe, sharing the stories of God's work. Her husband has already gone to be with the Lord, but she continues the work they pioneered and established. During the meeting, I was inspired by this spry, dynamic woman. Her countenance was full of beauty, and she glowed with the presence and glory of God. There was no mistaking it. Her passion for the Lord was deeply stirring.

I caught something that day. I definitely saw, in that beautiful woman of God, something that I wanted for my own life. I threw my lasso on it and asked the Lord to help me catch what this woman had. And should the Lord tarry, that is exactly how I want to live my life—to the full, even when I am a little old lady, singing His songs and taking His message around the world until I breathe my final breath. How about you?

I will sing to the LORD as long as I live.
I will praise my God to my last breath!
—Psalm 104:33 (NLT)

Willing Vessel

Words and Music
By Carolyn J. Vargas © 2013/ASCAP

Cracked and scarred through battle
Fragile in some ways
Yet so much stronger from the journey
Then I was in younger days
Lessons and experience
The wisdom that they bring
Compassion, understanding
For the hurting that I see

Lord, please use this willing vessel
To do one more thing for you
One more thing for you
In the vastness of your purpose
May you see my heart is true
To do one more thing for you
One more thing for you

Lord, I still remember
The day you called my name
And asked of me to follow you
And faithful to remain
You said I had a destiny
I've tried to do my part
In pressing forward to the goal
In pressing to the mark

You see that I am weary
Some days can be a stretch
But you know I am willing
You know I always give my best
I know that you have others
That are young and full of zeal
Yet I still have your promise
Of a place inside your will

To love you and to serve you
Is all that I desire
To follow where you lead me
My heart's passion
My heart's fire

Lord, please use this willing vessel
To do one more thing for you
One more thing for you
In the vastness of your purpose
May you see my heart is true
To do one more thing for you
One more thing for you

CHAPTER 7

Spring

Forget the former things;
do not dwell on the past.
—Isaiah 43:18 (NIV)

For I am about to do something new.
See, I have already begun! Do you not see it?
I will make a pathway through the wilderness.
I will create rivers in the dry wasteland.
—Isaiah 43:19 (NLT)

"For I know the plans I have for you," declares the Lord,
"plans to prosper you and not to harm you,
plans to give you a hope and a future."
—Jeremiah 29:11 (NIV)

For there is hope for a tree, if it is cut down,
that it will sprout again, and that its tender shoots will not cease. Though
its root may grow old in the earth, and its stump may die in the ground,
yet at the scent of water it will bud and bring forth branches like a plant.
—Job 14:7-9 (NKJV)

Chapter 7

Spring

There is nothing that looks more barren and dead to me than a tree in the winter (evergreens excluded). Stripped of their beautiful leaves, the outer bark faces the elements of the harsh winter weather to protect the life inside. Without the covering of leaves and fruit, the tree is exposed for all to see.

A tree looks so dead during the winter because it has become dormant, which is as close to death as it could possibly be while still living. Nearly everything in the tree has shut down or slowed to such a degree that it is asleep and barely functioning. It will not be awakened until there is a complete shift in the atmosphere and everything changes.

Perhaps you feel as if things on the inside of you are as near to being dead as they possibly can be. Take heart! The right shift in your atmosphere can change everything suddenly! Bring on the sunshine! Bring on the warmer and longer days! Bring on the rains that will get your root system activated again! Let's get that sap moving!

Many things contribute to the atmospheric shifts that bring a tree out of winter and into spring. I am no arborist, but my big God knows exactly what to do and how to change the atmosphere perfectly to make this possible. Just as He knows how to bring the trees to life again, He knows exactly how to shift the atmosphere in our personal lives, bringing us out of winter and into the wonderful season of spring.

Spring—ah, yes, spring. Just the sound of the word brings a smile to my face. Lovely visions of budding trees, green fields, and flowers pushing up through the soil come into my mind.

When I think about spring, I think about *transition*. Transition is certainly a part of moving from one season into another, but especially the process of moving from the cold, dark days of winter into the season of new beginnings. There is a stirring and a sense of eager anticipation as we perceive that things are changing. Spring is in the air! So much was stripped away during the winter that we may still feel a sense of vulnerability. Yet the hope of new days and the expectation of new beginnings encourage us onward when our more natural reaction might be to draw back.

One special spring that stands out in my memory occurred while living in England. That year, winter seemed to drag on and on forever. Then one day, I was driving down a little back road. Trees hung over the lane, and shafts of light were breaking through the gray skies, pouring through the trees and onto the road. Earlier, there had been a light rain, and everything the light touched had a brilliant shimmer. It was breathtaking. I drove that lane every day to take my daughter back and forth to school, but on this day, as I observed the sparkling wet road with the shafts of sunlight spilling through the trees, I saw something I had not seen the day before. The trees were filled with a stunning hue, tiny specks of color glistening brilliantly from the moisture of the rain.

Overnight, it seemed, the trees had budded and were announcing the arrival of spring. With my heightened awareness of the beauty surrounding me, I heard the

Lord whisper, saying, "The winter is over, and spring has arrived." That spring would prove to be a very productive season for me, as I wrote quite a lot of music all while surrounded by the most beautiful English countryside.

Watch for new beginnings. Stay alert to the many wonderful things the Lord has planned for your life, such as divine connections, open doors, fresh vision, inspiration, creativity, and much more. Be courageous to do things you have never done before, if you know the Lord is directing you. Be ready to put your hand to the plow, as there are fields that need to be planted. New life is surrounding you. Be on the lookout! Remember, everything changes quickly when spring arrives.

Spring

Words and Music
By Carolyn J. Vargas © 2013/ASCAP

The winter is over
I scarce can believe it
How long have I yearned for the spring
Now here at last
There are buds all around me
And beautiful pastures of green

Oh, what was I thinking
While deep in the winter
I thought that the spring
Would not come
Now here we are
With the beauty of springtime
Surrounded by God's faithful love
Surrounded by God's faithful love

Such hope is restored
In my heart; I can feel it
Refreshed—oh, renewed and revived
I'm swaying and dancing
And singing with laughter
Rejoicing, so thankful am I

Oh, what was I thinking
While deep in the winter
I thought that the spring
Would not come
Now here we are
With the beauty of springtime
Surrounded by God's faithful love
Surrounded by God's faithful love

Now what is the lesson
That we should be learning
From this lovely story of spring
Just never forget that the Lord
He is working
No matter what season we see

CHAPTER 8

It Wasn't Very Long Ago

You made all the delicate, inner parts of my body and knit me together in my mother's womb. Thank you for making me so wonderfully complex! Your workmanship is marvelous—how well we know it. You watched me as I was being formed in utter seclusion, as I was woven together in the dark of the womb. You saw me before I was born. Every day of my life was recorded in your book. Every moment was laid out before a single day has passed. How precious are your thoughts about me, o God. They cannot be numbered.
—Psalm 139:13-17 (NLT)

Children are a gift from the lord;
they are a reward from him.
—Psalm 127:3 (NLT)

Train up a child in the way he should go,
and when he is old he will not depart from it.
—Proverbs 22:6 (NKJV)

Chapter 8

It Wasn't Very Long Ago

One of the greatest gifts God has given me in this life is my beautiful daughter. I will never forget the miracle of her birth, and the joy of holding my newborn daughter in my arms for the first time. I kept gazing at her tiny fingers and marveling at how perfectly formed each little part of her body was. Her little face and bright, discovering eyes captivated me. I watched every expression with amazement and delight, so remarkable was God's glorious creation. An unexplainable love came over me for this precious, tiny baby, and my heart soared as I held this priceless gift.

Realization of the responsibilities ahead was sobering. So many needs would have to be met, from the very practical side of everyday care, to meeting the emotional needs of nurturing, and loving this beautiful child. It was easy to feel unequipped for such an important role. Yet in all things, the Lord promises to help us, giving wisdom and guidance along the way. And as always, He is faithful.

There is nothing like watching the growth of a child to make us more aware of the passing of seasons. From the first wobbly steps and the first words barely understood, we urge them on, and encourage them, cherishing every moment of cheerful fun and laughter shared together. Our hearts break over every tear they cry and every situation through which they struggle.

We are keenly aware of our own shortcomings as parents and the mistakes we make along the way. It's easy to reflect, in hindsight, as to how something could have been handled better. Many times, I would have loved to hit the rewind button and have a do-over. But those parenting years are a *one take only*. Thankfully, children are very resilient and eagerly respond when parents sincerely ask them to forgive them for their mistakes.

And so we give of what we have learned and pour the best of what we are into our precious gifts. We pray that they will learn, and become strong in the Lord as they grow up in a world that is filled with danger and pitfalls. Until the day arrives when they are launched out on their own, we do all that is possible to protect them from evil and guide them toward faith in God, knowing that He is the only one who can keep them.

It really doesn't seem that long ago that I cradled and rocked my little baby, singing her to sleep with tender lullabies. As I held her in my arms, I prayed for all that God had for her life and future.

My beautiful child is now a grown woman. She is out on her own, making her way in the world, living a busy and productive life. Where did the years go? Like other parents, my prayers for her have not ceased; that the Lord's hand will continue to be strong upon her, that He protect her, guide her, and direct her life, enabling her to reach her destiny in Christ.

It Wasn't Very Long Ago

Words and Music
By Carolyn J. Vargas © 2013/ASCAP

It wasn't very long ago
I held her in my arms
I whispered gentle, loving words
And sheltered her from harm
I looked into those big, bright eyes
And my heart sang a song
How could those years just slip away
It hasn't been that long

Story books and make-believe
Wonder on her face
What a joyful picture
Of your love and of your grace
The sound of her sweet laughter
The heartbreak of her tears
How could the time just slip away
What happened to the years

Oh, the teenage drama
Such lessons with each day
Does her heart belong to you (Lord)
To guide her in the way
Such a lovely beauty
Lord, shelter her from harm
The years are passing quickly now
Please keep her in your arms

Now a grown young lady
Her future in your hands
She stands before her destiny
I know you have a plan
Guide her to your purpose
Grant her dreams come true
Bless her with each passing year
May she live her life for you

CHAPTER 9

Blessings

So let's not get tired of doing what is good.
At just the right time we will reap a
harvest of blessing if we don't give up.
—Galatians 6:9 (NLT)

I will bless my people and their homes around my holy
hill. And in the proper season I will send the showers
they need. There will be showers of blessing.
—Ezekiel 34:26 (NLT)

The Lord will open the heavens,
the storehouse of his bounty, to send rain on your land
in season and to bless all the work of your hands.
—Deuteronomy 28:12a (NIV)

I wait for you, o Lord; you will answer, o Lord my God.
—Psalm 38:15 (NIV)

Those who sow in tears will reap with songs of joy.
—Psalm 126:5 (NIV)

Chapter 9

Blessings

I love to hear people share their testimonies of God's answer to prayer and the mighty miracles He has performed—difficult situations resolved, financial breakthroughs, and healing. Not only am I overjoyed for those who have experienced breakthroughs, but I also celebrate their victories with them. Their testimonies remind me that in the areas where I pray and trust the Lord, He is working to bring victory and blessing.

It's like a cool, refreshing breeze on a still, hot summer day when breakthrough comes. Everything inside begins to relax with a deep sigh of relief. A heaviness we didn't even know we carried is lifted. The victory is won, and everything works out. Before we know it, we may even start doing a little dance, singing and shouting with glee, or who knows what, as we respond in thanksgiving to the Lord. Our great God has intervened on our behalf, and we are so grateful.

It is important for us to share our testimonies of what God has done, what He is doing, and how He brought us through, so that we can bless and encourage one another. Oh, how it stirs up faith and refreshes the heart to be reminded that our God is God, faithful and true. He loves His children like a good papa would, and the concerns of His children are His concerns.

During one Christmas season, while leading worship for our fellowship in Germany, the Lord gave me a vision to share with the people gathered there. As we came together to worship and celebrate the birth of Christ, I saw the heavens open and the Lord release gifts that came packaged in an assortment of sizes and were covered in the most beautiful wrappings, adorned with jewels, bows, and ribbons. We came together to bless and honor the Lord. Unexpectedly, the Lord opened our eyes to see that *He* was pouring out blessings on *us*—answers to prayer, financial supply, spiritual gifts, healing, refreshing, talents, wonderful unexpected surprises and much more.

We may at times feel that the Enemy has set up blockades to hinder us from receiving. But be assured, as much as we want to receive all the Lord has for us, He wants us to receive it even more! What He poured out on us that day in Germany, He continues to pour out on His children around the world. So keep trusting, keep praying, and keep believing!

As we pray, trust, and wait on the Lord for certain breakthroughs to occur, let us not get so caught up in the problem that we lose sight of the many blessings of God all around us. It is easy to get distorted vision. It is easy to get bogged down, fixated, and stressed out over a certain need or situation that is unresolved and forget that the battle belongs to the Lord. It is easy to end up carrying on our own shoulders the heavy weight of the struggles of life, when we were never meant to. Most of the time, we can't do anything about these situations in our own natural ability. Yet we get all tangled up in fear and stress. And what is accomplished? Nothing!

The Scriptures tell us that we are to cast our cares on the Lord and trust Him. In the gospel of Luke, we read,

> *Can all your worries add a single moment to your life? And if worry can't accomplish a little thing like that, what's the use of worrying over bigger things? Look at the lilies and how they grow. They don't work or make their clothing, yet Solomon in all his glory was not dressed as beautifully as they are. And if God cares so wonderfully for flowers that are here today and thrown into the fire tomorrow, he will certainly care for you. Why do you have so little faith?*
> —Luke 12:25–28 (NLT)

Wow! Let us never forget that our God cares for us and works on our behalf. Although it is true that some prayers seem to take a long time to be answered, and even though we may feel as if God has forgotten our address, God is working. God specializes in turning around the most impossible situations, even when there doesn't seem to be even a hint that the impossible could be possible. Keep pressing on! I can assure you that the Lord has not forgotten your address. Breakthrough is on the way!

The blessings of God are all around us. Let us not lose our awareness of, and gratitude for all that the Lord has done and is doing for us every day. Believe me, even as I type this out, I am preaching a good sermon to myself. We really are blessed beyond measure.

> *We have all benefited from the rich blessings he brought to us—one gracious blessing after another.*
> —John 1:16 (NLT)

Carolyn Vargas

Give Him thanks! Let Him know how grateful you are. Thrive in the midst of all that God is doing. Sing a song. Dance a dance, and rejoice in the Lord, your maker.

For the LORD God is a sun and shield; the LORD bestows favor and honor; no good thing does he withhold from those whose walk is blameless.
—Psalm 84:11 (NIV)

Blessings

Words and music
By Carolyn J. Vargas © 2013/ASCAP

Coming down
All around
The beautiful, wonderful
Blessings of God
Long-awaited answers to prayer
Are coming down from heaven above

Healing rain
Joy for tears
Mercy, and hope now abound
The heavens are open
Time of refreshing
Mighty miracles surround

Restoration
Hearts renewed
Power and strength now abound
The heavens are open
Time of refreshing
Mighty miracles surround

Coming down
All around
The beautiful, wonderful
Blessings of God
Long-awaited answers to prayer
Are coming down from heaven above

CHAPTER 10

Seasons of Life

While the earth remains, seedtime and harvest,
cold and heat, winter and summer, and
day and night shall not cease.
—Genesis 8:22 (NKJV)

Those who live only to satisfy their own sinful nature will
harvest decay and death from that sinful nature.
But those who live to please the spirit
will harvest everlasting life from the spirit.
—Galatians 6:8 (NLT)

A time to plant and a time to harvest.
—Ecclesiastes 3:2b (NLT)

A good tree produces good fruit, and a bad tree
produces bad fruit. A good tree can't produce bad
fruit, and a bad tree can't produce good fruit.
So every tree that does not produce good fruit
is chopped down and thrown into the fire.
—Matthew 7:17–19 (NLT)

Chapter 10

Seasons of Life

A sense of the fullness of time can be perceived as one season comes to an end, and the shift into a new season begins. If we have moved well in response and in harmony with the flow of that season and the plan of God for our lives through that time, much has been accomplished.

The better we are at discerning the shifts and changes in our life's *atmosphere*, the better prepared we will be to transition and adjust to what is soon coming and move forward in God's plan. Failure to do so can cause us to resist what the Lord is doing, and we could easily find ourselves at odds with change, feeling uncomfortable, out of sorts, and out of sync with the Lord and His plan for our lives. This can sometimes cause a move in the wrong direction, or even delay what the Lord wants to do. But as we submit to the Lord, He will help us get back into His plan and flow.

When the cycles of our seasons bring us around to autumn, we become more aware of the fruit of our lives. It's harvest time! There are times when we sow, and there are times when we water, tend, and nurture. There are also times when we reap. Yes, all of our lives will bear fruit! The question is, what kind of fruit will it be? Will it be fruit that remains and makes a difference for the kingdom of God? Or will it be fruit riddled with worms and disease, not fit for nourishment, but only fit to be thrown into the fire: It is not in my nature to be hard, but it is important to be truthful and direct; we really will reap what we sow!

Like other seasons, we will cycle through autumn many times during our lives. Toward the second half of life, there seems to be a greater awareness of what harvest time means. As if there is an inward clock ticking, there is a need to know that we have accomplished something of value. If our focus is centered in Christ and God's eternal purpose, this inward stirring is simply a nudge from the Lord that reminds us to continue living as those who will one day give an account for our lives.

If a person's focus in life is not centered in Christ and God's eternal purpose, the inward stirrings that occur as harvest time nears can take on a distorted, disturbing response. We are all familiar with what is known as the *midlife crisis*. In one, a midlife crisis may manifest as adolescent behavior acted out in an effort to avoid the realization of the particular season the person is in. In another, it may show up as a workaholic who is determined to have a great accumulation of material goods to show as a harvest for his or her life. Certainly, there are plenty of other variations, but you get the idea.

I am not opposed to being financially blessed—far from it. We need to be financially blessed so that we can help move forward the plan and purpose of God on the earth. You have to have resources to do that. However, an accumulation of material goods is not the way to measure the fruit and value of a person's life. Remember, we are only stewards for a short time. All that we have belongs to God. And none of our material possessions go with us as we stand before the Lord, our maker. Material goods will not be the standard by which our harvests are measured.

There are many things we will sow through the course of a lifetime, but I can't write about harvest time without mentioning some of the most important things we have to sow—the words we speak! The words we speak have a lot to do with the lives we end up building, and the harvest we will eventually reap. The Bible is full of reminders that we are to be wise about the words we speak.

> *The tongue can bring death or life; those who love to talk will reap the consequences.*
> *—Proverbs 18:21 (NLT)*

> *He who guards his mouth and his tongue keeps himself from calamity.*
> *—Proverbs 21:23 (NIV)*

> *And so blessing and cursing come pouring out of the same mouth. Surely, my brothers and sisters, this is not right!*
> *—James 3:10 (NLT)*

There really is power in what we say! Our words will bring life or death, blessing or cursing. They will build up or tear down, and we will reap a harvest from the words we speak. (James 3)

Many times, I have realized that something thoughtless flew out of my mouth and injured someone. Oh, I would have loved to be able to take back those words, but it was too late. Sometimes we have the opportunity to capture the moment, and make an effort to repair the damage that was done by our injurious words, but other times, we are unable to. I have truly grieved when I discovered that I wounded someone with my words. Sadly, sometimes we aren't even aware that our words were hurtful, which cautions us even more to be watchful of what we say.

Carolyn Vargas

> *The words of the reckless pierce like swords,*
> *but the tongue of the wise brings healing.*
> *—Proverbs 12:18 (NIV)*

I find it especially heartbreaking that the importance of watching our words has become less and less valued in the days and times in which we now live. People have become so careless with their words, and say whatever they feel like saying without any regard as to how their speech might impact others. Swearing has become so conventional that we are rarely even shocked anymore by what we hear. People use toxic words in their communication more than ever.

> *The soothing tongue is a tree of life,*
> *but a perverse tongue crushes the spirit.*
> *—Proverbs 15:4 (NIV)*

I especially cringe inside when I hear parents in public places blast their little children with foul language, cursing at them and threatening them with verbal abuse. I have actually *felt* evil emanating from words poured out on a little, wide-eyed child. Is it any wonder our children are broken and have emotional problems? And why should we think it strange when little children spew out foul language themselves? This is what has been sown into them, and this is the harvest our society reaps.

> *May the words of my mouth and*
> *the meditation of my heart be pleasing to you,*
> *O LORD, my rock and my redeemer.*
> *—Psalm 19:14 (NLT)*

Ultimately, in the sunset of a person's life, the final harvest will begin to reveal itself as a summary of the life that he or she has lived and all that he or she has sown and reaped through the years. Yes, by God's grace, many things sown that would not bring forth good fruit are placed under the blood of Christ, as we have asked the Lord to forgive us and bring a crop failure. But we can't live our lives with a passive attitude, thinking we can indulge in willful sin and still have lives of fruitfulness in the Lord.

We all desire to feel that our lives are valuable and that our final harvest will bring forth fruit that remains. What will we see in our final harvest? Have we lived lives filled with the passion of God's purpose? Have we loved well? Have we worked hard to build meaningful relationships? Have we been faithful to God and His plan for our lives? If we have done these things, then we have sown that which will produce lasting fruit—a harvest that will stand for all eternity. Harvest time is coming!

Seasons of Life

Words and Music
By Carolyn J. Vargas © 2013/ASCAP

There is a feeling of change in the air
A sense of the fullness of time
A new season is close at hand
That will carve and shape our lives

Will it be the winds of winter
That we find safe shelter from
Will it be the hope of springtime
As we see the new buds come
Will it be the warm summer breeze
With joyful laughter sweet
Will it be the leaves of autumn
As we thank the Lord
For all we reap

The seasons of life will always come
There is no doubt they will
Sow the seeds of life well
For there will be a day
When we will reap
What we have sown

Winter winds
Buds of spring
Summer breeze
Autumn leaves

CHAPTER 11

I Will Say Farewell

I write these things to you who believe in the name
of the son of God so that you may know that
you have eternal life.
—1 John 5:13 (NIV)

I tell you the truth, those who listen to my message and
believe in God who sent me have eternal life.
They will never be condemned for their sins, but they
have already passed from death into life.
—John 5:24 (NLT)

Jesus said to her, "I am the resurrection and the life.
He who believes in me will live, even though he dies."
—John 11:25 (NIV)

Jesus told him, "I am the way, the truth, and the life.
No one can come to the father except through me."
—John 14:6 (NLT)

Chapter 11

I Will Say Farewell

Seated by my mother's hospital bed, I was keenly aware that she was in the final days of her life. I didn't feel in any way prepared for this experience. A lifetime of memories passed through my mind while at the same time filtering through my heart. I kept telling myself, *Stay focused; she needs your prayers and support. Deal with your emotions another time. Put them all in a box, and set them aside to process later. Right now, she needs you to be strong.* But try as I did, it wasn't that easy to shut down all of the feelings and flow. Outwardly, the tears were at a minimum, but inside, I felt a flood of intense emotions ready to break through at any moment. And so it is as we face the loss of those we love.

My first significant encounter with death was that of a childhood friend. We had been pals from grade school through high school. A year or so after high school, I faced the heartbreak of hearing that my friend was gone.

Standing by her casket at the funeral home, I looked into the face of my dear friend, and she appeared as beautiful as ever. But she wasn't there. The cascade of memories that flooded my mind—childhood laughter, mischief we had gotten into, and all the growing up that we did together—were to be filed away in my heart, as I would never again be able to speak of them with my dear friend.

Since that first experience years ago, many dear ones—both family and friends—have gone on to meet the Lord. It is a very hard part of the lives we live, to face the sorrow of such special people passing away. God never created us for death. That is most likely the reason we struggle with it so much.

For our loved ones who knew the Lord, we celebrate their going home to be with Him. But in our humanity, we still must deal with the sorrow of their absence and loss to our lives.

Closure is a word that is tossed around a great deal these days. After the passing of one special friend, I struggled quite a bit and found myself at the piano, crying out to the Lord. I guess I needed *closure*. I needed to release my loved one and the loss I experienced, along with my grief and sorrow, and be comforted by the Lord so that I could go on with my life. I played and I cried. I prayed, I played, and I cried some more! Little by little, my heart was able to put words to my inward struggle, and the Lord reached in to give me comfort. As His comfort came into my heart, I was reminded that my friend is in glory with Him, and one day, I will see her again. She completed her journey and ran her race well. No more pain! No more sorrow! No more sickness! No more struggle!

As I sang to the Lord, other special people in my life who had gone on to be with Him came to my thoughts. I realized and understood like never before what a homecoming it will be when my own time comes to pass from this natural, earthly realm into God's eternal, glorious heaven. Not only will I see my Jesus face-to-face, but all of my precious loved ones who have gone on before me will also be waiting there. What a day that will be!

I Will Say Farewell

Words and Music
By Carolyn J. Vargas © 2013/ASCAP

I will say farewell
Until we meet again
Upon that shore
Where sorrow is no more
Your journey now complete
You've crossed beyond the veil
To stand before
Our Savior and our Lord

Yet not far away
In my heart you stay
And I know that
We will be together one day

He will say, "Well done
Thou good and faithful one"
And give to you
The blessings you are due
Then others you will see
Down through eternity
The precious saints
That all have gone before

Yet not far away
In my heart you stay
And I know that
We will be together one day

I will say farewell
Until my time has come
When then at last
My journey is complete
I will see you again
My dear and precious friend
Upon that shore
Where sorrow is no more

CHAPTER 12

For a Brief Moment

The harvesters are paid good wages, and
the fruit they harvest is people brought to eternal life. What
joy awaits both the planter and the harvester alike!
—John 4:36 (NLT)

Teach us to realize the brevity of life,
so that we may grow in wisdom.
—Pslam 90:12 (NLT)

We are confident, I say, and willing
rather to be absent from the body,
and to be present with the Lord.
—2 Corinthians 5:8 (NKJV)

Chapter 12

For a Brief Moment

The years and seasons of our lives move along much more quickly than we could ever imagine. Life really is very short. In reality, our lives here on earth last for only *a brief moment*, as one pastor expressed in his sermon. I have pondered that little phrase, "a brief moment," over and over again.

Coupled with the brevity of life is the amazing significance that each life brings to our world. We are each just one person; yet every life is immeasurably valuable and has a part to play in God's wonderful plan. Just for a moment, think about how one person's life impacts many others. It is profound! One life intertwines with and impacts another life, which in turn impacts and intertwines with another, and then another, and so on. Each life makes a difference. Our lives are woven together in this way in God's eternal purpose, for the sake of others and for our sake.

Pause and remember all the people you have met and known. Each one has impacted your life in some way. Sure, there are the special key people who jump to the top of your list, but beyond those are so many others that counting them or even remembering them all through the span of a lifetime would be impossible. Our lives are to be impactful in that way. We are blessed to be a blessing for Christ's sake.

The awareness that life is brief reminds us of the importance of living our lives with intention, for the glory and purpose of God. Time is short and passes very quickly. As our final season comes to an end and our cycle of life on earth comes to a close, remember that this is not all there is.

> *For our dying bodies must be transformed into bodies that will never die; our mortal bodies must be transformed into immortal bodies. Then, when our dying bodies have been transformed into bodies that will never die, this Scripture will be fulfilled:*
> *"Death is swallowed up in victory.*
> *O death, where is your victory?*
> *O death, where is your sting?"*
> *—1 Corinthians 15:53–55 (NLT)*

From the beginning to the end, God is faithful! A home in His glorious heaven awaits those of us who have lived our lives in Christ, along with eternal reward for faithfully serving him. The promises of God forever hold true, and even as the last moments of our lives on earth approach, we can know that the Lord is there, and that our last breath will transition us from this natural realm into God's heavenly kingdom, where we will see our Savior face-to-face.

For a Brief Moment

Words and Music
By Carolyn J. Vargas © 2013/ASCAP

For a brief moment
For a brief moment in time

For a brief moment
For a brief moment, I am here

I am here to live my life
To live my life for you

And when I take my final breath
I will know your faithfulness
As I see you face-to-face
To lead me home

CHAPTER 13

Glory

Father, I want those you have given me to be
with me where I am, and to see my glory,
the glory you have given me because you
loved me before the creation of the world.
—John 17:24 (NIV)

In my father's house are many mansions:
if it were not so, I would have told you.
I go to prepare a place for you.
—John 14:2 (NKJV)

And God shall wipe away all tears from their eyes;
and there shall be no more death, neither sorrow, nor
crying, neither shall there be any more pain:
for the former things are passed away.
—Revelations 21:4 (NKJV)

And the city has no need of sun or moon,
for the glory of God illuminates the city,
and the lamb is its light.
—Revelation 21:23 (NLT)

Chapter 13

Glory

The final track on the album was completely unexpected, as it was never a planned part of the project. My producer, Mark Edwards, had been listening to the title track, "Lord of the Seasons," while I was out of the studio. While hitting various buttons, playing around with the mix, and different parts of the lead vocal tracks and the backing vocal tracks, Mark stumbled onto something that captured his attention.

The next morning, when I arrived back at the studio, the first thing Mark said was that he had something he wanted me to hear. It was a song within a song. What had caught Mark's attention quickly caught mine as well. There were layers of vocals that we had recorded throughout the song to add dimension and texture to the sound. When those vocal layers were played alone, without any accompanying instruments, they had a sound and presence that stood on their own.

I have often pondered the miraculous birth of this beautiful song. In the natural, it *seemed* to be accidental, but it wasn't! It was a song woven into a song by the Holy Spirit, with the sound of eternity in it. This surprising glimpse into the sound of eternity caused me to think a great deal about the song we each sing with our life. Our lives *are* songs that saturate everyone and everything around us—a song within a greater song that is meant to bring an orchestral type expression of God's divine, eternal sound into the earth. As we flow with the Holy Spirit, our lives harmonize and become one with that majestic, eternal song that is God's great song over all creation, and we bring glory to our Lord Jesus Christ, the King of Kings and Lord of Lords. When we take our last breath on earth and breathe our first breath in heaven, what a joy it will be to stand before the Lord face-to-face and present the song of our lives to Him as an offering of love and adoration.

I don't know for certain what heaven will look like or be like, but I have often pondered the mystery and grandeur of this wonderful place. We get little glimpses of what it might be like when reading Scripture: worship before the throne of God, angels, amazing colors, sounds we have never heard before, a city made of precious jewels, beauty and majesty beyond imagination, streets of gold, the river of life, a home that is prepared for us, and those we love who have gone on before waiting for us.

Regardless of what heaven is truly like, one thing I know for sure is that it is more beautiful than we could ever imagine and more wondrous than we could ever find words to express, as the presence of God, in all His love and glory, will saturate everything.

> *That is what the Scriptures mean when they say,*
> *"No eye has seen, no ear has heard, and*
> *no mind has imagined what God has prepared*
> *for those who love him."*
> *—1Corinthians 2:9 (NLT)*

Final Thoughts

*Hold firmly to the word of life;
then, on the day of Christ's return,
I will be proud that I did not run the race in vain
and that my work was not useless.
—Philippians 2:16 (NLT)*

This life the Lord has given us to live is sometimes referred to in Scriptures as a race. It is not a sprint, but a long-distance race or marathon, so you must pace yourself! As I share my final thoughts, I ask that you consider all that you need to complete such a race. I encourage you to ponder spiritual longevity.

*But my life is worth nothing to me unless I use it for
finishing the work assigned me by the Lord Jesus—
the work of telling others the Good News
about the wonderful grace of God.
—Acts 20:24 (NLT)*

We are often called upon to make better choices for ourselves so that we can live longer, healthier lives in the physical, but how about our spiritual lives? Are we making the best choices we can to ensure spiritual longevity—to be sure our faith stays fresh, vibrant, and full of passion throughout our lifetimes? If not, then let's ask ourselves why.

The Lord has many wonderful *God assignments* for you to fulfill during your lifetime and many great adventures for you to experience with Him. Spiritual longevity is a must! Don't get distracted, fall away, or drop out, but remain alert so that you can run your race well through the many seasons of your life. Let's stoke up that fire within, and forever keep it blazing. You want to finish your race just as you began it—strong and true, a faithful servant of the Lord Jesus Christ.

> *I have fought the good fight,*
> *I have finished the race,*
> *I have kept the faith.*
> *—2 Timothy 4:7, (NIV)*

Prayer of Salvation

If you have never had the opportunity to ask Jesus Christ into your heart as your personal Lord and Savior, now is your time. Simply ask Him to come into your heart and be the Lord of your life. His peace and love will flood you.

These words may be helpful as you pray your own prayer from the heart:

> *Dear heavenly Father,*
> *I believe that Your Son, Jesus the Christ, came in the flesh, was crucified on the cross for my sin, and rose from the dead by the power of Your Holy Spirit. I invite You now, Lord Jesus, to come into my heart. I ask You to forgive me and translate me out of the kingdom of darkness into Your glorious kingdom. I ask You to help and guide me, from this day forward and enable me to live my life for You. Amen.*

Other Materials By Carolyn Vargas

Music CDs

LORD OF THE SEASONS

THE BRIDE TO THE BRIDEGROOM

IN MY FATHER'S ARMS

To contact the author, please visit:
WWW.CAROLYNVARGAS.COM

For the vision is yet for an appointed time;
But at the end it will speak, and it will not lie.
Though it tarries, wait for it;
Because it will surely come,
It will not tarry.
—Habakkuk 2:3 (NKJV)